101 Facts About

PETS
101 Facts About
101 Facts About

101 FACTS ABOUT

BUDGERIGARS

Published by Ringpress Books Limited,
PO Box 8, Lydney, Gloucestershire,
GL15 4YN, United Kingdom.

Design: Sara Howell

First Published 2001
© 2001 RINGPRESS BOOKS LIMITED

ISBN 1 86054 241 7

Printed in Hong Kong through Printworks Int. Ltd

0 9 8 7 6 5 4 3 2 1

101 FACTS ABOUT

BUDGERIGARS

Julia Barnes

Ringpress Books

1 The budgerigar, with his beautifully-coloured feathers and cheeky character, is the most popular pet bird in the world.

2 The budgie is a member of the parrot family, and his original home is Australia. In the United States, budgerigars are often known as parakeets.

3 In the wild, large flocks of budgies fly together, searching for food. When Captain James Cook explored Australia in 1770, it was reported that the flocks were so large that they covered the sun as they passed.

4 When early settlers asked the native Aborigines the name of these little green-coloured birds, they replied "betchery-gah", which became known as budgerigar.

measure only 4 ins (10 cms) from head to tail-tip, whereas a pet budgie may measure up to 10 ins (25 cms).

7 All wild budgies are light green in colour, so they can blend in with their surroundings.

5 Many years later, when experts translated the Aborigine language, they discovered that the word meant 'good to eat'!

6 Wild budgies are much smaller than the pet budgies we can buy. They

8 Their nests are made in rotting tree branches. They hollow out a dark space where the female budgie (**hen**) can lay her eggs.

9 The first budgerigars reached Europe in 1840, and in 1870 the first all-yellow budgie was hatched in Belgium.

10 This was the start of a new trend in breeding budgies with different colours. There are now more than 60 different colours, plus many hundreds of patterns and colour combinations.

11 The four basic colours for budgerigars are blue, white, green and yellow.

12 There are different shades within each of these colours. For example, a blue budgie could be sky blue, cobalt blue, or mauve.

6

15 Some birds are bred with a fringe of feathers around the head. They are the **crested** variety (pictured left). The **tufted** budgerigar has a crest which sticks up at the front of his head.

13 All-yellow birds with red eyes are known as '**lutinos**', and birds that have no colouring are called '**albinos**'. They are totally white.

14 If a budgie has patches of yellow and green, or blue and white in its feathers, it is known as '**pied**'. No two pieds are exactly the same.

16 Breeders are still working to create new colours and patterns. The **spangled** variety (pictured right), where the budgie has a solid body colour and mottled wings, is a recent example.

17 All varieties of budgie have a similar temperament and most are equally easy to care for.

18 Budgerigars are warm-blooded. A budgie will pant to cool down, and will fluff up his feathers to keep warm.

19 The budgie's body is covered with small '**contour**' feathers. It has larger '**flight**' feathers at the back of the wings (pictured right). The tail is also made up of larger feathers.

20 Every so often a budgie will **moult**, which is a process of shedding his old feathers and growing new ones.

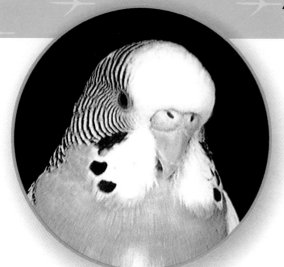

23 The budgie has a curved beak which he uses for cracking open seeds, preening (cleaning) feathers and also for climbing.

21 The sharp-eyed budgie can see much better than us. The eyes are placed on the sides of the head, so birds can see to the sides as well as to the front.

24 When your budgie goes to sleep, he will stand on one leg and tuck his head under his wing.

22 A budgie has three eyelids: an upper, a lower, and a third eyelid that he can pull across the eye from the side to protect it.

25 Budgerigars can be taught how to talk. Male birds (**cocks**) are better talkers than females (hens).

26 A budgie called Puck, who lived in California, USA, knew a recordbreaking 1,728 words before he died in 1994.

27 The most famous talking budgie was Sparkie Williams, who knew eight nursery rhymes and 500 different words.

28 A healthy budgerigar will live for seven to eight years, though some have been known to live longer.

29 The oldest recorded budgie was Charlie, who lived in London, UK, and reached the grand old age of 29.

30 The best age to buy a pet budgie is between seven and eight weeks when he is easiest to tame.

or a hen. Between three to four months, the cere changes from pale purple to blue in cocks, and to a brown colour in hens.

31 You can tell if a budgie is still a youngster (pictured above) if the black wavy patterning (**barring**) reaches down to the **cere**, which is the fleshy area above the beak.

33 You will need expert advice when you are choosing your budgerigar, so make sure you go to a shop that specialises in bird care.

32 It is not easy to tell whether a young budgie is a cock

35 The bird you buy should show the following signs of good health.

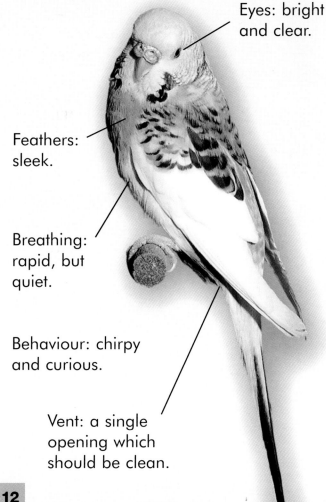

Eyes: bright and clear.

Feathers: sleek.

Breathing: rapid, but quiet.

Behaviour: chirpy and curious.

Vent: a single opening which should be clean.

34 If you want one of the more unusual varieties, you will need to go to a budgerigar breeder.

36 Your budgerigar will need a home, so you need to plan this well in advance.

37 Budgerigars will be happy living in a cage, an indoor enclosure (**flight**) which is big enough to fly around in, or they can live in an outside **aviary** (pictured below).

38 A budgerigar will be very lonely if he is kept on his own, so try to keep at least two budgies together.

39 When you are planning a home, go for the biggest you can afford (pictured above).

40 Remember, budgies fly from side to side, not upwards, so choose a cage that is as wide as possible.

41 Budgies love to climb, so buy a cage with horizontal bars to encourage exercise and prevent boredom.

42 The cage should not be in direct sunlight, and it should be in a place that is free from cold blasts of air, or your budgies could catch a chill.

43 If you plan to keep a large number of birds, a garden aviary provides a wonderful, natural home.

46 The perches must be of different widths. If they are all the same, your budgie will get sore feet.

44 An aviary has an outdoor flight, and a weatherproof shelter where the budgerigars can go at night or in bad weather.

47 You can use a branch from a fruit tree. Do not use branches from any other types of tree because some are poisonous.

45 Whatever type of home you provide, it will need to be fitted with a number of perches.

48 The best type of floor covering in a cage is ready-made sand sheets which are available in most pet stores.

49 You will also need to provide a food container. Make sure you do not position this under a perch or the food will be spoiled by droppings.

50 A fresh supply of water should be provided by a bottle attached to the cage.

51 Budgies are active birds and will enjoy using a ladder to get from perch to perch.

52 There are lots of budgie toys you can buy, or you can provide a table tennis ball, or some empty cotton reels threaded on string, which will provide hours of fun.

feathers (pictured below) – which is known as **preening** – unless they can wet their feathers.

53 Choose a different toy every day to give your budgies plenty of variety.

54 Bathtime is fun-time for budgies. They enjoy splashing around in a shallow saucer of warm water.

55 Bathing also serves a very useful purpose. Budgies cannot clean their

56 There are a number of seed mixes especially for budgerigars. They are made up of a mixture of different seeds.

57 Try to buy a mix that contains red rape, linseed, or niger, as well as the round-shaped millet seeds, and the oval-shaped canary seeds.

58 A budgie will break open a seed with his beak so that he can get to the inner part, the '**kernel**'. The outer part, the '**husk**', is not eaten.

59 You must clear away the husks every day, or your budgies will start getting hungry if they cannot find the new seed because it is buried by old husks.

60 Green food provides variety in the diet. Favourites include grass that is going to seed, dandelion, groundsel and chickweed. Make sure they have not been sprayed with any poisonous chemicals.

61 Some budgies like gnawing at a piece of apple or carrot, jammed between the bars of the cage.

62 Fresh millet (pictured right) is enjoyed, but do not feed too much or your budgies will get fat.

63 Every budgie home needs a bowl of grit (pictured below). This is used by the budgies to help digest their food.

64 Budgies have no teeth, so they swallow the seed whole. This is mashed down in the **gizzard**, which needs grit in order to function.

65 To keep your budgerigars healthy, they must have the correct minerals in their diet. A cuttlefish bone (pictured above), attached to the side of the cage, will provide calcium, and you will also need to provide a mineral block (right).

66 Apart from feeding your budgies, the most important job is to keep their home clean.

67 Every day, you should change the sand sheets from the bottom of the cage, clear away the seed husks, and throw away any other food that has been left. You will also need to check the water bottle.

68 Every week, clean all the contents of the cage. Wipe the bars of the cage and replace the floor covering. Check that the bowl of grit is topped up.

69 Budgerigars are hardy little birds, and with a good diet and clean housing, they will suffer few health problems.

70 It is a good idea to find a vet in your area that specialises in treating birds.

71 Keep a check on your budgie's nails. They should wear down naturally if you provide a variety of different perches.

72 If they grow too long, ask your vet or an experienced birdkeeper to trim them for you.

73 If you provide cuttlefish bone, your budgie's beak should not grow too long.

74 If the beak is too long, your budgie will not be able to pick up and de-husk seeds, so this condition needs urgent attention. Ask your vet to clip the beak for you.

21

75 If you are introducing a second budgie to your home, he should be kept in a separate cage for the first couple of weeks.

76 This will give him a chance to adjust to the new surroundings and you can be certain that he is healthy before he comes into contact with other birds.

77 Allow the budgies to see and hear each other from a distance, and then move the two birds into the same cage.

78 You will be keen to make friends with your budgies, but give them a day to settle before you attempt to handle them.

79 On the second day, you can start finger-training (pictured above). Start by opening the cage door with one hand, and blocking up the opening with the other hand so that the budgie cannot escape.

80 Put one hand in the cage, holding a piece of millet spray, and place it near the perch so that your budgie can easily hop on to it.

81 Hold your hand very still and wait for your budgie to pluck up the courage to make a move.

82 Eventually, the budgie will hop on to your hand and will nibble the millet.

83 Do not rush this 'making friends' stage. The longer you spend getting your budgie's trust and confidence, the tamer he will become.

86 Before you allow your budgie to fly free, you must make sure the room is completely safe, and has no possible dangers.

84 When your budgie has accepted your hand coming into the cage, try using your finger as a perch.

85 Do not allow a budgie out of the cage until he is finger-tame. The budgie needs to see your finger as a safe landing place that he is happy to return to.

87 Close all doors and windows, and draw the curtains. A budgie can easily panic and fly into a pane of glass.

88 Make sure fireplaces are well guarded, and electric fans should be switched off. If you have a dog or cat, make sure they are kept well away.

89 When your budgie gets used to going out of his cage, he will thoroughly enjoy the chance to fly and to explore.

90 When you are ready for your budgie to return to the cage, encourage the bird to hop on to your finger. Then you can take the bird back to the cage and transfer him to a perch.

91 Sometimes a budgie will get wise, and will fly off just before you get to the cage. You will need to be very patient, and use lots of treats to tempt your budgie to go back into his cage.

92 A budgerigar should also get used to being handled, as well as just perching on your finger. This is important if your budgie needs to receive any treatment.

93 The correct way to hold a budgie is to enclose his body with one hand, holding his head with your thumb and forefinger at each side. The budgie will feel safe and secure – and he cannot peck you.

95 It takes quite a long time for a budgie to pick up his first word, but when he gets the idea, new words are learnt more quickly.

94 Budgerigars are good talkers, but you will need to spend time talking to your budgie to bring out his talents. Start with a single word, such as the budgie's name, and repeat it again and again.

97 Repeating words and short sentences is the key to teaching your budgie to talk. If you get fed up with saying the same things all the time, you can make a tape and play it to your budgie.

96 When your budgie repeats a word, make sure you have a tasty food reward – a piece of carrot or apple – ready to offer.

98 One of the most useful things you can teach your budgie is your address. If, by any chance, your budgie gets lost, you have a good chance of finding him again.

99 You can train your budgie to perform some simple tricks, such as climbing up a ladder, or ringing a bell on a toy.

100 Use your finger to show what you want your budgie to do, and, in time, he will learn to copy you.

101 Spend time talking to your budgie, teaching him tricks and watching him at play. Lively, friendly and intelligent, the budgie is one of the most rewarding pets to keep.

GLOSSARY

Albino: a white bird with no colouring.

Aviary: an outside enclosure that is big enough for birds to fly in.

Barring: black, wavy patterning which reaches down to the fleshy area above the beak.

Cere: the fleshy area above the beak.

Cock: a male bird.

Contour feathers: small feathers that cover the body.

Crested: a type of budgie that has a fringe of feathers around the head.

Flight feathers: large feathers at the back of the wings.

Hen: a female bird.

Husk: The outer part of a seed, which is not eaten.

Indoor flight: an indoor enclosure that is big enough for birds to fly in.

Keratin: the beak is made of keratin, which is a substance rather like our fingernails.

Kernel: the inner part of a seed.

Lutino: an all-yellow bird with red eyes.

Moult: a process of shedding old feathers.

Pied: a bird with patches of colour on the wings.

Spangled: a solid body colour with mottled wings.

Tufted: a type of budgie that has a crest of feathers sticking up at the front of his head.

MORE BOOKS TO READ

All About Your Budgerigar
Bradley Viner
(Ringpress Books)

Pet Owner's Guide to the Budgerigar
Stan and Barbara Moizer
(Ringpress Books)

Budgerigars (Junior Pet Care)
Zuza Vrbova
(TFH Publications)

Parakeets (Junior Pet Care Series)
Z Vrbova, S Miller, H Nicholas,
R McAulay and Sandra Stotsky
(Chelsea House Publishing Library)

 # WEBSITES

Pet budgies
www.birds.about.com/pets/birds/
library/blbudgie.htm

Parrots UK
www.parrotparrot.com/budgies/

Sammy bird
www.sammybird.com/parrots/
budgies/budgies.htm

Budgerigars.com
www.budgerigars.com/

To find additional websites, use a reliable search engine to find one or more of the following key words: **budgerigars**, **parakeets**, **pet birds**.

INDEX